Date Thy Self

DR. TANDY NANCE

About The Author

As the Founder and CEO of Redesign Your Life, LLC. Dr.Tandy Nance is a highly accomplished and dedicated Metaphysician, Certified Holistic Life Coach, International Author, and motivational Speaker. With over 18 years of experience in the mental health field, Dr. Tandy has amassed an impressive array of academic qualifications, including a Bachelor's degree in Criminal Justice, a Master's degree in Counseling Studies, a Master's degree in Business Administration, and a Doctorate in Metaphysical Humanistic Science.

Dr. Tandy is also the self-published author of "The Diva Code" a guide to leveling up designed to encourage self-improvement, the motivational self-help book "Boundaries+Clarity=Peace" which is designed to assist individuals who are struggling to create boundaries and gain the clarity necessary to make positive changes in their lives, "Your Body Is Your Castle" a six-week guide to eating healthier and having a positive body image, and co-author of "Forgiveness Is Therapeutic" created to emphasize the power of forgiveness, healing, and moving forward. Her books aim to empower people to find peace and fulfillment in their lives.

Copyright Page

Copyright © 2023 Dr. Tandy Nance

Dedication

I dedicate this book to my ancestors, whose presence has been a vital part of my healing journey.

-Dr. Tandy

INTRODUCTION

Welcome to "Date Thyself: How to Release the Cycle of Toxic Relationships." This compelling book explores the power of self-love and transformation. Breaking free from toxic relationships is a challenging journey that demands time and conscious effort. To begin this journey, you must make a deliberate choice to let go of harmful patterns, negative energy, and past pain. By doing so, you choose to no longer be a prisoner of the past.

Holding onto anger and resentment keeps you trapped in disempowering emotions, preventing you from living fully in the present. Releasing these emotions is a commitment to change, and it takes practice. If you're struggling to break free from the cycle of toxic relationships, this book will provide the guidance you need to move toward healing. It will show you how to be honest with yourself, vulnerable, and aware of the steps needed to transform your energy and attract healthier connections.

All I ask is that you approach this journey with an open mind and an open heart.

Dr. Tandy

*"The moment that you start to wonder
if you deserve better, you do"*

-Unknown

Chapter 1
Introduction

"The more you love yourself, the less nonsense you tolerate."

-Dr. Tandy

The Journey Begins

Embarking on the journey of self-discovery and personal growth is a courageous and transformative decision. It is a commitment to understanding oneself on a deeper level, to unraveling the layers of experiences, emotions, and beliefs that shape our lives. This journey is not just about finding answers but about asking the right questions: Who am I? What do I truly want? How can I create a life filled with love, joy, and fulfillment?

In the context of relationships, self-discovery becomes even more crucial. Many of us find ourselves trapped in repetitive cycles of toxic relationships, wondering why we keep attracting the same kind of people and enduring the same kinds of pain. These patterns are not mere coincidences but reflections of our internal state—our energy signature.

By choosing to embark on this journey, you are taking the first step towards breaking free from these patterns. You are acknowledging that the key to transforming your relationships lies within you. This book, "Date Thyself: How to Break the Cycle of Toxic Relationships," is your guide to understanding and transforming your energy signature, so you can attract healthier and more fulfilling relationships into your life.

My Personal Story: From Broken to Empowered

I was married and divorced twice, and my life felt like it was spiraling out of control. I was overweight, tipping the scales at over 170 pounds. While that might not sound like much, on my 5'1" frame, those 170 pounds felt overwhelming. I was a single mother, feeling broken, insecure, and like a complete failure.

Six years into my first marriage, my husband joined my father in our family business—a business started by my grandfather, who was the first black bail bondsman in San Antonio. But what seemed like a promising partnership soon turned into a nightmare. My husband got my father's secretary pregnant. We get divorced, and I did what many women do—I started feeling rejected, less than, and convinced myself there was something inherently wrong with me.

In that state of brokenness and insecurity, I unknowingly manifested and attracted someone into my life who felt the exact same way, if not worse, about themselves. I literally divorced the pot and married the frying pan! I ignored all the red flags just to feel validated, seeking solace in someone as damaged as I felt.

This pattern of attracting toxic relationships wasn't merely a stroke of bad luck; it was a manifestation of my inner turmoil. My energy signature, shaped by feelings of rejection, insecurity, and inadequacy, drew similar energies into my life. Each failed relationship reinforced my negative beliefs about myself, creating a vicious cycle that seemed impossible to break.

The Journey of Self-Discovery

Self-discovery is the foundation of personal growth. It involves exploring your innermost thoughts, feelings, and desires, and gaining clarity about who you are and what you want from life. This process requires honesty, vulnerability, and a willingness to face uncomfortable truths about yourself.

For me, Dr. Tandy, the journey of self-discovery began with a profound sense of dissatisfaction and a desire for something more. I felt stuck in a cycle of unfulfilling relationships, constantly repeating the same mistakes and experiencing the same disappointments. This sense of dissatisfaction was a signal from my inner self, urging me to look within and make the necessary changes.

Self-discovery is not a one-time event but an ongoing process. It involves continuous reflection, learning, and growth. As I peeled back the layers of my identity, I uncovered hidden fears, limiting beliefs, and unresolved traumas that had been influencing my behavior and choices. By addressing these issues; I began to heal, Redesign my Life, and transform my energy signature.

The journey of self-discovery empowered me to take control of my life. It helped me recognize my strengths, embrace my weaknesses, and make conscious choices that align with my true self. In the context of relationships, self-discovery enabled me to understand my needs, set healthy boundaries, and attract partners who resonate with my authentic energy.

Breaking Free from Toxic Cycles

Toxic relationships can have a profound impact on your emotional and mental well-being. They drain your energy, erode your self-esteem, and leave you feeling trapped and helpless. Breaking free from these cycles is essential for your personal growth and happiness.

Toxic cycles often stem from deep-seated patterns and unresolved issues within ourselves. These patterns may originate from childhood experiences, past traumas, or learned behaviors. Without addressing these underlying issues, we are likely to repeat the same mistakes and attract the same types of toxic partners.

Breaking toxic cycles requires a conscious effort to change your energy signature. It involves identifying and releasing negative patterns, healing past wounds, and cultivating a positive and healthy mindset. This process is not easy, but it is incredibly rewarding. As you transform your energy, you will begin to attract healthier relationships and experience a greater sense of fulfillment and joy.

One of the most important steps in breaking toxic cycles is learning to love and value yourself. When you date yourself, you prioritize your own needs and desires, and you set the standard for how you expect to be treated by others. Self-love is the foundation of healthy relationships. It empowers you to make choices that honor your worth and well-being.

By breaking toxic cycles, you are not only improving your own life but also creating a positive ripple effect on those around you. Healthy relationships inspire and uplift others, creating a supportive and nurturing environment for everyone involved. As you transform your energy and attract positive relationships, you contribute to a collective shift towards love, respect, and harmony.

In the next chapters, we will explore the concept of energy signatures and how they influence your relationships. You will learn practical techniques to identify and transform your energy signature, so you can break free from toxic cycles and attract the love and happiness you deserve. Remember, the journey begins with you. Date thyself, love thyself, and watch your life transform.

"The greatest discovery in life is self-discovery. Until you find yourself you will always be someone else. Become yourself."

-MYLES MUROE

Chapter 2
Understanding Energy Signatures

What Are Energy Signatures?

The Concept of Energy Signatures

At the core of our being, we are all composed of energy. This energy is not just physical but extends to our thoughts, emotions, and overall state of being. An energy signature is essentially the unique vibrational frequency that each person emits. It is a combination of our mental, emotional, and spiritual states, and it influences how we interact with the world around us.

Think of your energy signature as your personal radio frequency. Just as a radio station broadcasts specific frequencies that can be picked up by radios tuned to the same frequency, our energy signatures send out vibrations that are picked up by others with matching or resonant frequencies. This is why certain people feel an instant connection or repulsion towards each other, often without any logical explanation.

How Energy Signatures Influence Our Relationships

Our energy signatures play a crucial role in the types of relationships we attract. If you often find yourself in toxic relationships, it might be a reflection of your current energy signature. Negative emotions like fear, insecurity, or anger can lower your vibrational frequency, making you more likely to attract individuals with similar negative energies. Conversely, positive emotions such as love, joy, and confidence raise your frequency, attracting healthier and more positive relationships.

Understanding your energy signature means recognizing the patterns and emotions that you consistently emit. It requires a deep level of self-awareness and honesty about your inner state. By becoming conscious of your energy signature, you can begin to make intentional changes that will shift your vibrational frequency and, consequently, the types of people and experiences you attract into your life.

If this is what your energy signature looks like...

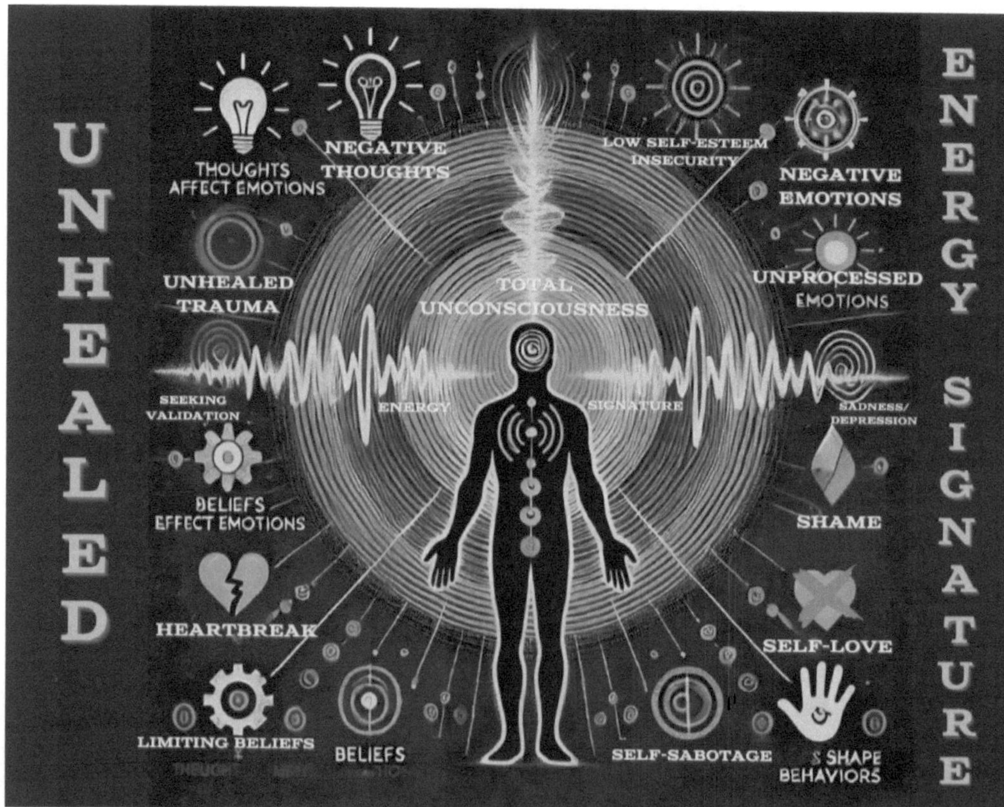

There is absolutely no way you can attract someone with an energy signature that looks like this...

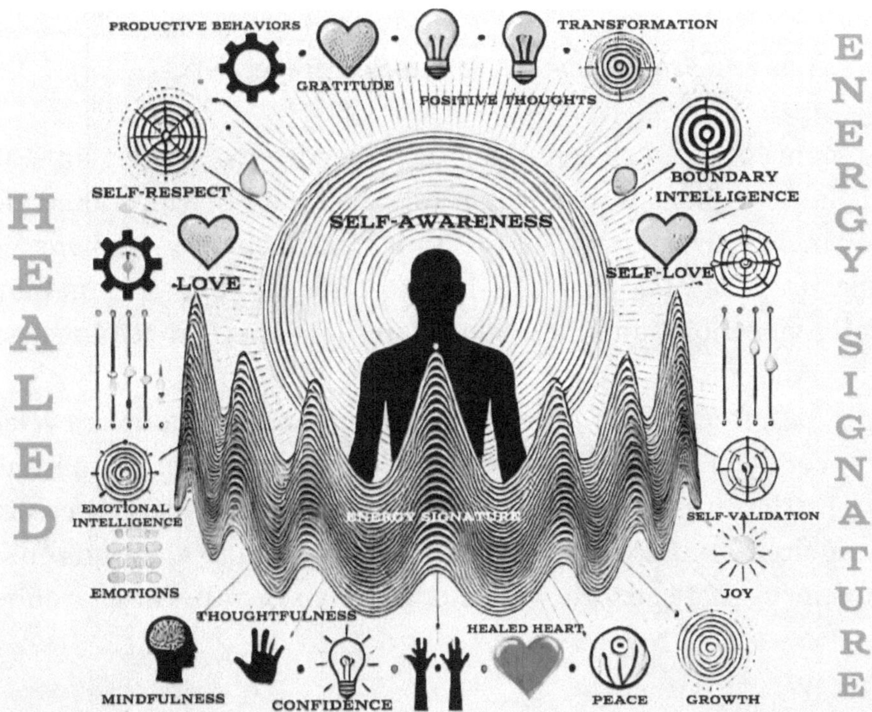

Your partner's energy signature will look very similar to yours. However, it may be caused by different negative experiences, thoughts, beliefs, and emotions.

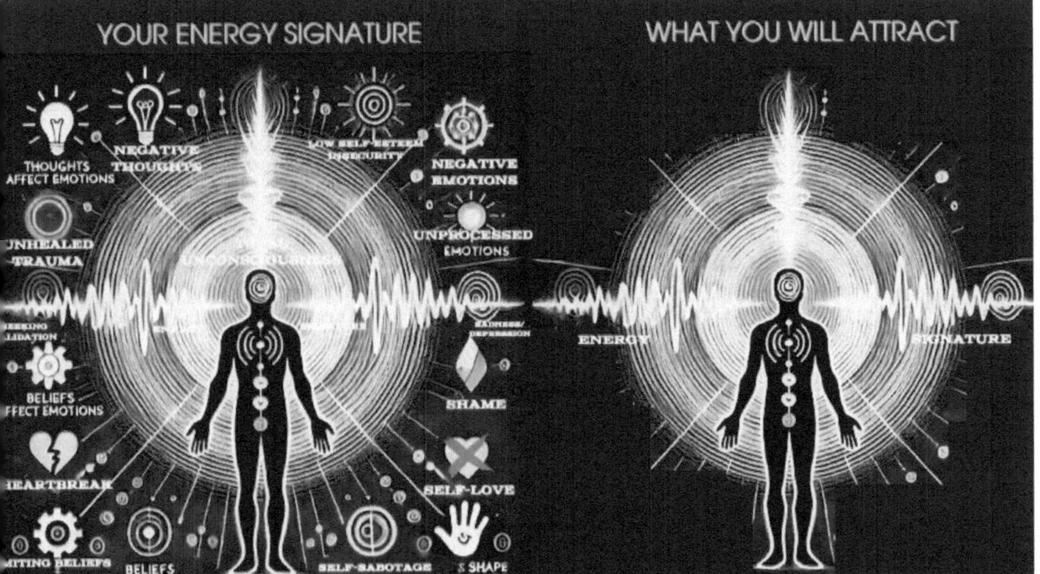

The Science Behind Energy

Vibrations and Frequencies: A Scientific Perspective

The concept of energy signatures is deeply rooted in the principles of physics, particularly in the study of vibrations and frequencies. Everything in the universe, including humans, is made up of atoms that are in constant motion. This motion creates vibrations, and these vibrations have specific frequencies.

In physics, frequency refers to the number of vibrations or cycles per second of a wave. These frequencies can be measured in hertz (Hz). Just as musical notes have different frequencies that create harmonious or dissonant sounds, our thoughts and emotions emit frequencies that can either harmonize or clash with those around us.

For example, emotions like love and joy have been found to produce higher frequencies, while fear and anger produce lower frequencies. This scientific understanding of frequencies helps explain why we feel more energized and uplifted around certain people and drained or agitated around others.

How Thoughts and Emotions Affect Our Energy

Our thoughts and emotions are powerful creators of our energy signature. Positive thoughts and emotions generate high-frequency vibrations, while negative thoughts and emotions produce low-frequency vibrations. This is not just a metaphorical concept but a measurable phenomenon.

Studies have shown that positive emotions can increase the coherence and strength of our electromagnetic field, which extends beyond our physical body. This field interacts with the fields of others, influencing how we feel in each other's presence. When we maintain a positive energy signature, we not only feel better ourselves but also positively affect those around us.

On the other hand, negative thoughts and emotions can disrupt our energy field, leading to physical and emotional imbalances. Chronic stress, anxiety, and negative thinking patterns can lower our vibrational frequency, making us more susceptible to attracting toxic relationships and negative experiences.

By becoming aware of our thoughts and emotions and actively working to shift them towards positivity, we can change our energy signature. Techniques such as meditation, mindfulness, and emotional regulation are effective ways to elevate our vibrational frequency and improve the quality of our relationships.

Understanding energy signatures is the first step toward transforming your relationship patterns. By recognizing the vibrations you emit and taking steps to elevate them, you can break the cycle of toxic relationships and attract the positive, loving connections you deserve. In the next chapter, we will delve into how to identify your current energy signature and uncover the patterns that may be holding you back.

Chapter 3
Identifying Your Current Energy Signature

"The first step to personal growth is the ability to make an honest assessment of where you currently are."

-UNKNOWN

SELF-ASSESSMENT

Understanding your current energy signature is the first step toward transforming your relationships. Self-assessment involves taking an honest look at your thoughts, emotions, and behaviors to identify the energy you are emitting. This process can reveal patterns and blocks that might be attracting toxic relationships into your life.

Tools and Exercises to Identify Your Energy Signature

Journaling: Start by keeping a daily journal where you record your thoughts, emotions, and experiences. Reflect on your interactions with others and note any recurring themes or patterns. This practice helps you become more aware of your internal state and how it influences your relationships.

Meditation and Mindfulness: Regular meditation and mindfulness practices can help you tune into your energy signature. Spend a few minutes each day in quiet contemplation, observing your thoughts and feelings without judgment. This will help you become more attuned to your inner vibrations and recognize any negative patterns.

Emotional Check-Ins: Set aside time throughout the day to check in with your emotions. Ask yourself how you are feeling and why. Identify any negative emotions and consider what might be triggering them. This practice helps you stay connected to your emotional state and understand how it affects your energy signature.

Feedback from Others: Sometimes, others can see patterns in us that we might miss. Ask trusted friends or family members for feedback on your behavior and relationships. Be open to their insights and consider how their observations align with your self-assessment. Also, you can seek professional help from a therapist or certified life coach such as Dr. Tandy, an expert in several energy healing techniques.

Recognizing Patterns in Past Relationships

Examining your past relationships can provide valuable insights into your energy signature. Look for recurring themes and patterns in your interactions and experiences. Consider the following questions:

- What types of people do you tend to attract?
- Are there common issues or conflicts that arise in your relationships?
- How do your relationships typically begin and end?
- What role do you usually play in your relationships (e.g., caregiver, peacemaker, victim)?

By identifying these patterns, you can begin to understand how your energy signature influences your relationships. This awareness is the first step towards making positive changes.

Energy Blocks and Toxic Patterns

Energy blocks are unresolved emotional or psychological issues that disrupt the natural flow of your energy. These blocks can lower your vibrational frequency and attract toxic relationships. Understanding and addressing these blocks is crucial for transforming your energy signature.

Common Energy Blocks That Lead to Toxic Relationships

1. **Fear of Abandonment:** This block often stems from childhood experiences of neglect or loss. It can lead to clinginess, jealousy, and insecurity in relationships, pushing partners away and creating a self-fulfilling prophecy of abandonment.

2. **Low Self-Esteem:** If you don't believe you are worthy of love and respect, you may attract partners who reinforce this belief. Low self-esteem can manifest as settling for less, tolerating abusive behavior, or constantly seeking validation from others.

3. **Unresolved Trauma:** Past traumas, such as abuse or betrayal, can leave deep scars on your energy signature. These unresolved issues can lead to distrust, emotional numbness, and difficulty forming healthy attachments.

4. **Negative Beliefs About Relationships**: If you hold negative beliefs about relationships, such as "all men/women are untrustworthy" or "love always leads to pain," these beliefs can shape your experiences. Your energy signature will reflect these beliefs, attracting partners and situations that confirm them.

How These Blocks Manifest in Our Lives

Energy blocks can manifest in various ways, affecting your behavior, emotions, and overall well-being. Here are some common manifestations:

- **Repetitive Relationship Patterns:** Continuously finding yourself in similar toxic relationships is a clear sign of energy blocks. These patterns persist until the underlying issues are addressed.

- **Emotional Reactivity:** Overreacting to minor issues or experiencing intense emotions disproportionate to the situation indicates unresolved emotional blocks. This reactivity can strain relationships and push partners away.

- **Physical Symptoms:** Energy blocks can also manifest as physical symptoms, such as chronic pain, fatigue, or illnesses. These symptoms often reflect unresolved emotional issues and stress.

- **Self-Sabotage:** Engaging in behaviors that undermine your happiness and success, such as pushing people away, neglecting self-care, or making destructive choices, can indicate deep-seated energy blocks.

Identifying your current energy signature and recognizing the blocks that influence it is a crucial step in transforming your relationships. By using the tools and exercises provided, you can gain a deeper understanding of your energy and begin to make conscious changes. In the next chapter, we will explore the power of self-love and how dating yourself can help you shift your energy signature and attract healthier relationships.

Chapter 4
The Power of Self-Love

"Fall in love with taking care of yourself. Fall in love with the path of deep healing. Fall in love with becoming the best version of yourself but with patience, with compassion, and respect for your journey"

-S. MCNUTT III

Date Thyself

The Concept of Date Thyself

Date Thyself is an empowering practice that involves prioritizing your own needs, desires, and well-being. It means treating yourself with the same love, respect, and care you would offer a romantic partner. This concept is about building a strong, healthy relationship with yourself, which lays the foundation for attracting positive and fulfilling relationships with others.

When you date yourself, you acknowledge your worth and take deliberate steps to nurture your mind, body, and spirit. This practice helps you become more attuned to your own needs and desires, and it reinforces the message that you are deserving of love and happiness.

Activities and Practices for Self-Love

1. Solo Adventures: Plan regular outings and activities that you enjoy. This could be anything from a solo movie night, a hike in nature, visiting a museum, or dining at your favorite restaurant. These experiences allow you to spend quality time with yourself and enjoy your own company.

2. Pamper Yourself: Treat yourself to a spa day, a relaxing bath, or a new hairstyle. Pampering yourself is a powerful way to show self-love and care. It helps you feel valued and appreciated, boosting your self-esteem.

3. Pursue Your Passions: Engage in hobbies and activities that ignite your passion and creativity. Whether it's painting, writing, gardening, or playing a musical instrument, doing what you love nourishes your soul and reinforces your sense of self-worth.

4. Practice Mindfulness: Spend time in meditation or mindfulness practices to connect with your inner self. Mindfulness helps you stay present and aware of your thoughts and feelings, fostering a deeper understanding and acceptance of yourself.

5. Set Boundaries: Learn to say no to things that drain your energy and yes to things that uplift you. Setting healthy boundaries is a crucial aspect of self-love, as it ensures that you prioritize your own well-being and protect yourself from negative influences.

BUILDING A POSITIVE RELATIONSHIP WITH YOURSELF

Affirmations and Self-Care Routines

Affirmations are positive statements that help you challenge and overcome negative thoughts and self-doubt. By repeating affirmations regularly, you can reprogram your mind to focus on your strengths and potential. Here are some examples of affirmations for self-love:

- "I am choosing to be worthy of love and respect."
- "I am choosing to be enough just as I am."
- "I am choosing happiness and fulfillment."
- "I am choosing to love and accept myself unconditionally."

Incorporate these affirmations into your daily routine by saying them out loud in front of a mirror, writing them down in a journal, or setting reminders on your phone. The more you reinforce these positive messages, the more they will become ingrained in your subconscious mind.

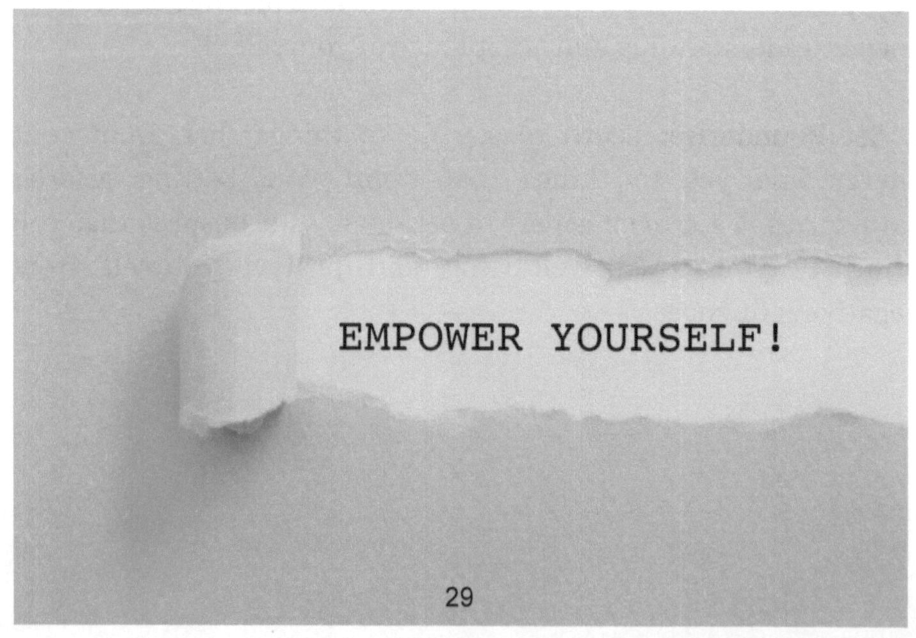

Journaling and Self-Reflection Exercises

Journaling is a powerful tool for self-discovery and personal growth. It allows you to explore your thoughts and feelings, gain insights into your behaviors, and track your progress over time. Here are some journaling prompts to help you build a positive relationship with yourself:

What do I love about myself?
What are my strengths and talents?
What makes me feel happy and fulfilled?
How can I show myself more love and compassion?
What boundaries do I need to set to protect my well-being?

Spend time each day or week reflecting on these prompts and writing down your thoughts. Journaling helps you gain clarity about your needs and desires, and it encourages self-awareness and self-acceptance.

Self-Reflection Exercises

1. **Gratitude Practice:** Write down three things you are grateful for each day. Focusing on gratitude shifts your mindset to a positive perspective and helps you appreciate the good in your life.
2. **Mindful Breathing:** Practice mindful breathing exercises to center yourself and reduce stress. Close your eyes, take deep breaths, and focus on the sensation of the breath entering and leaving your body.
3. **Positive Visualization:** Visualize yourself achieving your goals and living your best life. Imagine the feelings of joy and satisfaction that come with your success, and let these positive emotions guide your actions.

Building a positive relationship with yourself through self-love practices is essential for breaking the cycle of toxic relationships. When you date yourself and prioritize your well-being, you set the standard for how you expect to be treated by others. In the next chapter, we will explore practical steps to shift your energy signature and attract healthier relationships. Remember, the journey to self-love begins with you. Date thyself, love thyself, and watch your life transform.

"A Shift of Energy is Always Followed By A Change in Reality"

-PANACHE DESAI

Chapter 5
Shifting Your Energy Signature

CLEARING NEGATIVE ENERGY

Techniques for Cleansing and Protecting Your Energy

Clearing negative energy is a crucial step in shifting your energy signature. Negative energy can accumulate from various sources, including past traumas, toxic relationships, and daily stress. Here are some effective techniques to cleanse and protect your energy:

Energy Healing Techniques: Various energy healing methods can help cleanse and balance your energy. These techniques include Emotion/Body/Belief Code, hypnotherapy, and holistic life coaching. Emotion/Body/Belief Code involves identifying and releasing trapped emotions, beliefs, and bodily sensations that contribute to negative energy. Hypnotherapy uses guided relaxation and focused attention to achieve a heightened state of awareness, allowing you to address and heal deep-seated issues. Holistic life coaching integrates physical, emotional, and spiritual aspects to promote overall well-being and energy balance. Dr. Tandy is certified in all of these techniques, ensuring you receive professional and effective energy healing.

Salt Baths: Taking a bath with Epsom salts or Himalayan pink salt can help draw out toxins and negative energy from your body. Add a few drops of essential oils like lavender or eucalyptus for added relaxation and cleansing.

Grounding: Spend time in nature, walk barefoot on grass, or sit by a tree to connect with the earth's energy. Grounding helps stabilize and balance your energy, releasing any negativity back into the earth.

Meditation and Visualization Exercises

Meditation and visualization are powerful tools for cleansing and protecting your energy. Here are some exercises to incorporate into your routine:

White Light Meditation: Sit in a comfortable position and close your eyes. Visualize a bright white light surrounding your body, starting from the top of your head and gradually enveloping your entire being. Imagine this light cleansing and purifying your energy, removing any negativity and filling you with peace and positivity.

Chakra Cleansing Meditation: Focus on each of your seven chakras, starting from the root chakra at the base of your spine to the crown chakra at the top of your head. Visualize each chakra as a spinning wheel of light, clearing away any blockages and restoring balance to your energy centers.

Protective Shield Visualization: Close your eyes and take a few deep breaths. Visualize a protective shield of light forming around your body. This shield acts as a barrier, preventing any negative energy from entering your personal space while allowing positive energy to flow freely.

Raising Your Vibration

Practices to Elevate Your Energy

Raising your vibration involves adopting practices that elevate your emotional and mental state. When your vibration is high, you attract positive experiences and people into your life. Here are some practices to help you raise your vibration:

Gratitude Practice: Begin each day by listing three things you are grateful for. Gratitude shifts your focus from what you lack to what you have, creating a positive mindset that attracts more of what you appreciate.

Mindfulness: Practice being present in the moment. Mindfulness helps you stay connected to your inner self and reduces stress, promoting a higher vibrational state. Spend a few minutes each day in mindful breathing or simply observing your surroundings.

Positive Thinking: Challenge negative thoughts and replace them with positive affirmations. For example, if you catch yourself thinking, "I am not good enough," replace it with, "I am capable and worthy of love and success." Consistently practicing positive thinking can significantly elevate your vibration.

Acts of Kindness: Perform random acts of kindness for others. Whether it's helping a neighbor, volunteering, or simply offering a smile, these actions create a ripple effect of positivity that elevates your own energy.

Healthy Lifestyle Choices: Nourish your body with nutritious foods, exercise regularly, and get enough sleep. A healthy body supports a healthy mind and spirit, contributing to a higher vibration.

The Role of Gratitude, Mindfulness, and Positive Thinking

Gratitude, mindfulness, and positive thinking are foundational practices for raising your vibration. Here's how they play a crucial role:

Gratitude: Practicing gratitude shifts your focus from what is missing in your life to what is abundant. This change in perspective attracts more positive experiences and amplifies your overall sense of well-being. Gratitude helps you appreciate the present moment and fosters a sense of contentment and joy.

Mindfulness: Being mindful allows you to fully engage with the present moment, reducing anxiety and stress about the past or future. Mindfulness helps you become more aware of your thoughts and feelings, enabling you to consciously choose positivity and release negativity.

Positive Thinking: Positive thinking transforms your internal dialogue and influences your energy signature. By consistently focusing on positive thoughts and affirmations, you reprogram your mind to see opportunities instead of obstacles, fostering a more optimistic and high-vibrational outlook.

Shifting your energy signature involves both clearing negative energy and raising your vibration. By incorporating these practices into your daily life, you can create a positive and powerful energy signature that attracts healthy relationships and fulfilling experiences. In the next chapter, we will explore practical steps to identify and transform energy blocks that may be hindering your progress. Remember, the journey to a higher vibration begins with conscious and consistent effort.

"Your value doesn't decrease based on someone's inability to see your worth."

-ZIG ZIGLAR

Chapter 6

Attracting Healthy Relationships

Understanding What You Deserve

Setting Healthy Boundaries

Healthy relationships are built on mutual respect and understanding. One of the key elements of cultivating such relationships is setting healthy boundaries. Boundaries are essential for protecting your emotional, physical, and mental well-being. They help define your limits and communicate your needs and expectations to others.

Identify Your Boundaries: Start by reflecting on what makes you feel comfortable and safe in relationships. This includes physical space, emotional interactions, and mental engagement. Recognize areas where you feel drained or disrespected and pinpoint what needs to change.

Communicate Clearly: Once you have identified your boundaries, communicate them assertively and clearly to others. Use "I" statements to express your needs, such as, "I need some alone time to recharge," or "I feel uncomfortable when…"

Be Consistent: Consistency is crucial in maintaining boundaries. Stand firm on your limits and do not waver, even if others try to challenge them. This consistency will reinforce your boundaries and ensure that they are respected.

Respect Others' Boundaries: Just as you set your own boundaries, be mindful and respectful of the boundaries set by others. This mutual respect fosters a healthy and balanced relationship.

Recognizing Your Worth and Value

Understanding your worth and value is fundamental to attracting healthy relationships. When you recognize your own value, you set a standard for how you expect to be treated. This self-awareness and self-respect act as a powerful filter, allowing only those who appreciate and respect you to enter your life.

Self-Reflection: Spend time reflecting on your strengths, achievements, and qualities that make you unique. Write them down and revisit this list regularly to remind yourself of your worth.

Self-Compassion: Practice self-compassion by treating yourself with kindness and understanding, especially during times of failure or self-doubt. Replace self-criticism with positive affirmations and supportive self-talk.

Celebrate Yourself: Acknowledge and celebrate your accomplishments, no matter how small. Recognizing your successes reinforces your sense of self-worth and boosts your confidence.

Surround yourself with people who uplift and support you. Positive relationships reinforce your sense of value and encourage you to maintain high standards in all your interactions.

Manifesting Positive Relationships

The Law of Attraction and Relationships

The law of attraction posits that like attracts like. Your thoughts, feelings, and beliefs send out vibrational frequencies that attract similar energies into your life. By aligning your energy with the type of relationship you desire, you can manifest positive and healthy connections.

Visualize Your Ideal Relationship: Spend time visualizing the type of relationship you want. Imagine the qualities, values, and dynamics of this relationship in vivid detail. This visualization helps you align your energy with your desired outcome.

Set Intentions: Clearly define your intentions for a healthy relationship. Write them down and affirm them regularly. Statements like, "I am worthy of a loving and respectful relationship," or "I attract partners who value and appreciate me," reinforce your goals.

Focus on Positivity: Maintain a positive mindset by focusing on what you want rather than what you lack. This positive focus raises your vibrational frequency and attracts similar positive energies.

Let Go of Limiting Beliefs: Identify and release any limiting beliefs that may be blocking you from attracting healthy relationships. Replace these beliefs with empowering ones that support your goals.

How to Attract People Who Match Your New Energy Signature

As you transform your energy signature through self-love, positive thinking, and boundary setting, you will naturally attract people who resonate with your new frequency. Here are steps to attract relationships that match your elevated energy signature:

Be Authentic: Embrace your true self and express your authenticity in all your interactions. Authenticity attracts genuine connections and repels those who do not align with your true self.

Engage in Activities You Love: Participate in activities and communities that reflect your interests and values. This increases the likelihood of meeting like-minded individuals who share your passions and energy.

Practice Patience: Attracting the right people takes time. Be patient and trust that the universe is aligning things in your favor. Avoid settling for less out of impatience or fear of being alone.

Stay Open and Receptive: Keep an open mind and heart to new possibilities and connections. Sometimes, the right people come into your life in unexpected ways. Stay receptive to the flow of life and be ready to embrace new relationships.

Maintain High Standards: As you attract new relationships, continue to uphold your standards and boundaries. Ensure that new connections respect and align with your values and energy.

By understanding what you deserve and using the law of attraction to manifest positive relationships, you can create a life filled with love, respect, and fulfillment. The journey to attracting healthy relationships begins with recognizing your worth, setting boundaries, and aligning your energy with your desires. In the next chapter, we will delve into maintaining your new energy signature and ensuring lasting positive changes in your relationships. Remember, the power to attract the love you deserve lies within you. Date thyself, love thyself, and watch your relationships transform.

Chapter 7
Practical Steps to Change Your Energy Signature

"Pain serves a purpose. Without it, you are at risk. If you cannot feel it, you cannot heal it."

-DR. TANDY

DAILY PRACTICES

Morning and Evening Routines to Maintain a High Vibration

Starting and ending your day with high-vibrational routines sets a positive tone for your entire day and ensures a restful and rejuvenating night. Here are some practices to incorporate into your morning and evening routines:

Morning Routines

Gratitude Practice: Begin your day by listing three things you are grateful for. This simple practice shifts your mindset to a positive frequency and attracts more good into your life.

Meditation: Spend 5-10 minutes in meditation. Focus on your breath, visualize a successful and joyful day ahead, or use positive affirmations to set an uplifting tone for the day.

Positive Affirmations: Recite affirmations that align with your goals and desired energy. Examples include, "I am worthy of love and happiness," "I attract positive and supportive relationships," and "Today, I embrace joy and abundance."

Physical Movement: Engage in some form of physical activity, such as yoga, stretching, or a quick workout. Physical movement raises your energy levels and sets a dynamic pace for the day.

Healthy Breakfast: Nourish your body with a healthy breakfast. Opt for foods that fuel your body and mind, such as fruits, whole grains, and proteins.

Evening Routines

Reflection and Gratitude: Reflect on your day and identify positive moments or achievements. Write down three things you are grateful for that happened during the day.

Mindfulness Practice: Engage in a mindfulness practice such as deep breathing, gentle yoga, or a calming activity like reading or journaling to unwind and release any stress.

Visualization: Before bed, spend a few minutes visualizing your goals and dreams. Imagine them as if they are already happening, and feel the emotions associated with achieving them.

Disconnect from Technology: Turn off electronic devices at least an hour before bed to allow your mind to relax and prepare for restful sleep.

Create a Peaceful Environment: Ensure your sleeping environment is calm and conducive to rest. Use soft lighting, soothing scents, and comfortable bedding to create a sanctuary for sleep.

Incorporating Energy Work into Your Daily Life

Integrating energy work into your daily routine helps maintain a high vibrational frequency and supports continuous personal growth. Here are some practical ways to do this:

Regular Energy Cleansing: Use techniques like listening to high-frequency music, salt baths, or sound healing regularly to cleanse and refresh your energy.

Use Crystals: Carry protective and healing crystals such as amethyst, clear quartz, or rose quartz. Place them around your living space to enhance positive energy flow.

Positive Environment: Surround yourself with positive influences. This includes spending time with supportive people, consuming uplifting content, and creating a clutter-free, inspiring living space.

Mindful Consumption: Be mindful of what you consume, both physically and mentally. Opt for nourishing foods and avoid negative media or conversations that lower your vibration.

Daily Affirmations: Incorporate affirmations throughout your day. Write them on sticky notes and place them where you will see them, or set reminders on your phone.

Healing Past Wounds

Addressing and Healing Trauma

Healing past wounds is essential for shifting your energy signature. Unresolved traumas can block your energy and attract negative experiences. Here are steps to address and heal trauma:

Acknowledge the Trauma: The first step to healing is acknowledging that the trauma exists. Denial or suppression only prolongs the healing process. Accept your experiences and the impact they have had on you.

Seek Professional Help: Consider working with a therapist or certified life coach who specializes in trauma. Professional guidance can provide you with tools and techniques to process and heal your wounds. Dr. Tandy is a certified practitioner in Emotion/Body/Belief Code, hypnotherapy, and holistic life coaching, offering expert guidance and support to help individuals navigate their healing journeys effectively.

Practice Self-Compassion: Be gentle with yourself. Healing takes time and involves ups and downs. Treat yourself with kindness and understanding throughout the process.

Express Your Emotions: Find healthy ways to express your emotions. This could be through journaling, art, music, or talking with a trusted friend, therapist, or life coach.

Engage in Healing Modalities: Explore various healing modalities such as hypnotherapy, Emotion/Body/Belief Code, or holistic life coaching. Dr. Tandy is certified in these techniques and can guide you through the healing process.

Forgiveness and Letting Go

Forgiveness is a powerful step in healing past wounds and releasing negative energy. Holding onto resentment and anger keeps you tethered to the past. Here are steps to practice forgiveness and let go:

Understand Forgiveness: Recognize that forgiveness is for your own healing and not necessarily for the benefit of those who hurt you. It does not mean condoning their actions but freeing yourself from the emotional burden.

Forgive Yourself: Often, we are hardest on ourselves. Acknowledge any mistakes you've made, learn from them, and forgive yourself. This self-forgiveness is crucial for moving forward.

Release Resentment: Identify the individuals or situations you need to forgive. Write a letter expressing your feelings, even if you do not send it. This act of writing can be cathartic and help release pent-up emotions.

Practice Letting Go: Letting go is a conscious decision to release the past. Use visualization techniques to imagine cutting the energetic cords that bind you to the trauma. Visualize yourself stepping into a future free from the past's hold.

Embrace New Beginnings: Focus on the present and future rather than dwelling on the past. Engage in activities that bring you joy and fulfillment, and surround yourself with positive influences.

Dr. Tandy has dedicated her career to helping individuals heal and transform their lives. In her book, "Forgiveness . Is Therapeutic," Dr. Tandy delves deeply into the concept of forgiveness, providing insights and practical tools for understanding and practicing forgiveness.

In "Forgiveness Is Therapeutic," Dr. Tandy emphasizes that forgiveness is a gift you give yourself. It is a crucial step towards healing and emotional freedom. The book offers strategies to recognize and release the burdens of anger and resentment, helping readers to let go and move forward with a lighter heart and a clearer mind.

By adding Dr. Tandy's teachings on forgiveness into your journey, you can achieve profound healing and transformation, allowing you to attract healthier, more positive relationships into your life.

When incorporating these daily practices and addressing past wounds, you can effectively change your energy signature. These steps will help you maintain a high vibrational frequency, attract positive experiences, and create the life you desire. In the next chapter, we will explore how to maintain your new energy signature and ensure lasting positive changes in your relationships and life. Remember, the journey to a higher vibration begins with conscious and consistent effort.

Chapter 8

Maintaining Your New Energy Signature

" Don't fall back into
your old patterns. Toxic habits and
behaviors always try to sneak back in
when you're doing better.
Stay focused."

-MARCANDANGEL

STAYING ON TRACK

Even with a transformed energy signature, life will present challenges and setbacks. It's essential to have strategies in place to navigate these difficulties while maintaining your positive energy.

Acknowledge and Accept: When setbacks occur, acknowledge your feelings without judgment. Accept that challenges are a part of life and an opportunity for growth.

Stay Grounded: Ground yourself through practices like deep breathing, meditation, or spending time in nature. Grounding helps you stay centered and reduces the impact of stress.

Reflect and Learn: Take time to reflect on the setback. What can you learn from this experience? How can it help you grow? Viewing challenges as learning opportunities shifts your perspective to a more positive one.

Maintain Your Routine: Stick to your daily routines, especially those that help elevate your energy, such as gratitude practices, affirmations, and physical exercise. These routines provide stability and comfort during tough times.

Seek Support: Don't hesitate to reach out for support from friends, family, or a professional. Sharing your experiences and receiving encouragement can lighten your emotional load.

Practice Self-Compassion: Be kind to yourself. Recognize that everyone faces challenges and that it's okay to struggle. Treat yourself with the same compassion you would offer to a friend in a similar situation.

Continuing Personal Growth and Self-Improvement

Personal growth is an ongoing journey. To maintain your new energy signature, continually seek opportunities for self-improvement and growth.

Set Goals: Regularly set personal and professional goals that challenge you and inspire growth. Break them down into manageable steps and celebrate your progress.

Lifelong Learning: Stay curious and open to learning new things. This could be through reading, taking courses, attending workshops, or exploring new hobbies.To help you maintain your new energy signature and continue your journey of self-love and personal growth, I have added a 21-Day Reflection Journey.

Reflect Regularly: Periodically reflect on your journey, your achievements, and areas for improvement. Self-reflection helps you stay aware of your progress and maintain your commitment to growth.

Embrace Change: Be open to change and new experiences. Embracing change rather than resisting it can lead to unexpected opportunities and growth.

Self-Care: Prioritize self-care to maintain your physical, emotional, and mental well-being. A well-balanced self-care routine supports continuous growth and a high-energy signature.

SURROUNDING YOURSELF WITH POSITIVITY

Building a Supportive Community

The people you surround yourself with significantly impact your energy. Building a supportive community can help you maintain your new energy signature and encourage your continued growth.

Seek Like-Minded Individuals: Connect with people who share your values, interests, and positive outlook on life. Join groups, clubs, or online communities that resonate with your goals.

Nurture Positive Relationships: Invest time and energy in relationships that uplift and support you. Surround yourself with people who encourage your growth and celebrate your successes.

Set Boundaries: Protect your energy by setting boundaries with individuals who drain you or bring negativity into your life. It's essential to prioritize relationships that contribute positively to your well-being.

Give and Receive Support: Be an active participant in your community. Offer support and encouragement to others, and be open to receiving help when you need it. This mutual support strengthens bonds and enhances positive energy.

Stay Connected: Regularly engage with your community through social events, conversations, and shared activities. Staying connected fosters a sense of belonging and support.

The Impact of Environment and Relationships on Your Energy

Your environment and the relationships you maintain play a crucial role in your energy signature. Here's how to optimize both for positive energy:

Create a Positive Living Space: Ensure your home environment is clean, organized, and filled with things that bring you joy. Use elements like plants, natural light, and uplifting decor to enhance the positive energy in your space.

Mindful Consumption: Be mindful of the media and content you consume. Choose uplifting, educational, and inspiring content over negative or stressful media.

Energy Cleansing: Regularly cleanse your living space using techniques like smudging, sound healing, or simply opening windows to let in fresh air and sunlight.

Practice Gratitude: Foster a culture of gratitude within your relationships. Express appreciation for the people in your life and encourage them to do the same.

Positive Communication: Engage in positive and constructive communication. Focus on uplifting conversations and avoid gossip or negative talk.

Maintaining your new energy signature requires conscious effort and commitment. By staying on track with personal growth, surrounding yourself with positivity, and being mindful of your environment and relationships, you can sustain the high vibrational frequency you have worked so hard to achieve. In the final chapter, we will explore real-life transformations and success stories, offering inspiration and practical advice for your continued journey. Remember, the power to maintain your positive energy lies within you. Date thyself, love thyself, and watch your energy continue to shine.

Chapter 9
Real-Life Transformations

"Sharing your story is not just about recounting events; it's about illuminating your journey, inspiring others, and finding strength in your own narrative."

-DR. TANDY

SUCCESS STORIES

Testimonials from Individuals Who Have Transformed Their Lives

Real-life transformations are powerful testaments to the effectiveness of changing one's energy signature. Here are some inspiring stories from individuals who have successfully transformed their lives through Dr. Tandy's guidance and the Redesign Your Life and Date Thy Self Program.

Jasmine's Journey to Self-Love

Jasmine had always struggled with low self-esteem and unhealthy relationships. After participating in the Redesign Your Life Program and learning about the importance of self-love from Dr. Tandy, she decided to embark on a journey of self-discovery. By incorporating daily affirmations, mindfulness practices, and setting healthy boundaries, Jasmine began to see a significant shift in her life. She now radiates confidence and has attracted a loving, supportive partner. Jasmine says, "Learning to love myself was the best decision I ever made. It changed my entire outlook on life and relationships."

Michael's Healing Process

Michael carried the weight of past traumas that affected his relationships and self-worth. Seeking help, he worked with Dr. Tandy through the Redesign Your Life Program to address his wounds using hypnotherapy and the Emotion/Body/Belief Code. This process allowed Michael to release deep-seated negative energy and embrace forgiveness. Today, Michael is not only in a healthy relationship but also mentors others on their healing journeys. "Healing my past was challenging, but it opened the door to a future filled with love and positivity," Michael shares.

Sophia's Transformation Through Gratitude

Sophia found herself constantly surrounded by negativity and toxic relationships. After joining the Redesign Your Life Program and learning from Dr. Tandy, she decided to focus on gratitude and mindfulness. By keeping a gratitude journal and practicing meditation, Sophia gradually shifted her energy signature. This transformation helped her build a supportive community and improve her overall well-being. Sophia advises, "Start small with daily gratitude. It has a ripple effect that can transform every aspect of your life."

Lessons Learned and Tips for Others on the Same Journey

From these success stories, several key lessons and tips emerge:

1. Consistency is Key: Regularly practicing gratitude, mindfulness, and self-care leads to lasting change.

2. Seek Support: Don't hesitate to reach out for professional help or connect with like-minded individuals.

3. Patience: Transformation takes time. Be patient and kind to yourself throughout the journey.

4. Embrace Change: Be open to new experiences and willing to let go of the past.

5. Celebrate Small Wins: Acknowledge and celebrate your progress, no matter how small it may seem.

YOUR STORY

Share Your Journey

Your journey is unique and valuable. Sharing your experiences can inspire and support others on similar paths. Here are ways to share your story:

Write About It: Start a blog or journal to document your journey. Sharing your thoughts and progress can be therapeutic and motivating.

Join Support Groups: Engage with online or local support groups where you can share your experiences and learn from others.
Social Media: Use social media platforms to connect with a broader audience and share your transformation journey.

Public Speaking: Consider speaking at events or workshops to share your story and inspire others.

Creating a Support Network

Building a supportive network is crucial for sustained growth and transformation. Here's how to create and nurture your support network:

1. Connect with Like-Minded Individuals: Seek out communities that align with your values and goals. These connections can provide encouragement and accountability.

2. Be Open and Vulnerable: Sharing your struggles and successes fosters deeper connections and mutual support.

3. Offer Support: Be an active member of your network by offering help and encouragement to others.

4. Celebrate Together: Celebrate milestones and achievements within your support network to reinforce positive progress.

"Redesigning your life is an act of courage, where you envision your dreams, embrace change, and craft a future that reflects your true self."

-DR. TANDY

Chapter 10
Conclusion
Redesigning Your Life

EMBRACING A NEW YOU

Celebrating Your Growth and Transformation

Take a moment to reflect on your journey and celebrate how far you've come. Embracing your new self involves recognizing and honoring the progress you've made. Celebrate your achievements, both big and small, and acknowledge the hard work you've put into transforming your energy signature.

Reflect on Your Journey: Take time to look back at where you started and appreciate the growth you've experienced.

Celebrate Milestones: Recognize and celebrate important milestones along your path to self-love and healthy relationships.

Reward Yourself: Treat yourself to something special as a reward for your dedication and perseverance.

The Ongoing Journey of Self-Love and Healthy Relationships

Remember that the journey of self-love and cultivating healthy relationships is ongoing. It requires continuous effort, reflection, and growth. Embrace the process and remain committed to nurturing your well-being and positive energy.

Stay Committed: Keep practicing the habits and routines that support your high vibration.

Keep Learning: Stay open to new experiences, knowledge, and growth opportunities.

Adapt and Evolve: Be flexible and willing to adapt as you continue to evolve on your journey.

Looking Forward

Future Goals and Continued Personal Development

As you move forward, set new goals that inspire and challenge you. Focus on continued personal development and strive to enhance your well-being and relationships.

Set New Intentions: Regularly set new intentions and goals that align with your evolving self.

Seek Growth Opportunities: Look for opportunities to learn and grow, whether through courses, workshops, or new experiences.

Maintain a Growth Mindset: Embrace challenges as opportunities for growth and remain open to change.

Encouragement for the Road Ahead

Your journey is a testament to your strength and resilience. Embrace the road ahead with confidence and optimism. Remember, you have the power to create a life filled with love, joy, and positive energy.

Believe in Yourself: Trust in your ability to overcome challenges and achieve your goals.

Stay Positive: Maintain a positive outlook and focus on the good in your life.

Enjoy the Journey: Take time to appreciate and enjoy the journey itself, not just the destination.

FINAL THOUGHTS

The journey to breaking the cycle of toxic relationships begins with you. It is a deeply personal and transformative process that requires self-awareness, commitment, and courage. By understanding and transforming your energy signature, you take control of the energy you emit and, consequently, the types of people and experiences you attract into your life.

Building Loving, Healthy Relationships

As your energy signature shifts, so does your external reality. You begin to attract relationships that reflect your new, elevated energy. These relationships are characterized by mutual respect, love, and support. You find yourself surrounded by people who uplift you, share your values, and contribute positively to your life.

Healthy relationships thrive on clear communication, mutual understanding, and respect for boundaries. By embodying these qualities yourself, you set a standard for how you expect to be treated. This attracts partners who respect and honor you, leading to fulfilling and balanced relationships.

The Most Important Relationship: With Yourself

The foundation of all positive changes in your life is the relationship you have with yourself. Self-love is the cornerstone of a high vibrational energy signature. When you prioritize your well-being, practice self-compassion, and treat yourself with kindness and respect, you set the tone for all other relationships in your life.

Date Thyself means investing time and effort into understanding your needs, desires, and passions. It means celebrating your achievements, forgiving your mistakes, and continuously striving for personal growth. The stronger and healthier your relationship with yourself, the more capable you are of building and sustaining healthy relationships with others.

Date Thyself, Love Thyself

The phrase "date thyself" is a call to action. It encourages you to take the time to know and love yourself deeply. When you date yourself, you engage in activities that bring you joy, practice self-care, and invest in your personal development. This practice not only enriches your life but also reinforces your self-worth and confidence.

Loving yourself is about recognizing your inherent value and treating yourself with the same love and respect you wish to receive from others. It's about setting boundaries, pursuing your passions, and nurturing your mind, body, and spirit. When you love yourself fully, you radiate a positive energy that naturally attracts loving and respectful relationships.

Watch As You Redesign Your Life

Transformation is both an internal and external process. As you change your energy signature and cultivate self-love, you'll notice significant shifts in your life. Toxic relationships will fall away, making room for healthier connections. Your self-esteem and confidence will grow, and you'll find yourself achieving goals and dreams that once seemed out of reach.

This journey is about more than just attracting the right people; it's about creating a life that reflects your true self. It's about living authentically, pursuing your passions, and experiencing the joy and fulfillment that come from being aligned with your highest self.

Remember, the journey of transformation and self-love is ongoing. Continue to date thyself, love thyself, and nurture your energy signature. Embrace the changes, celebrate your growth, and watch as your life redesigns in a beautiful and unexpected ways.

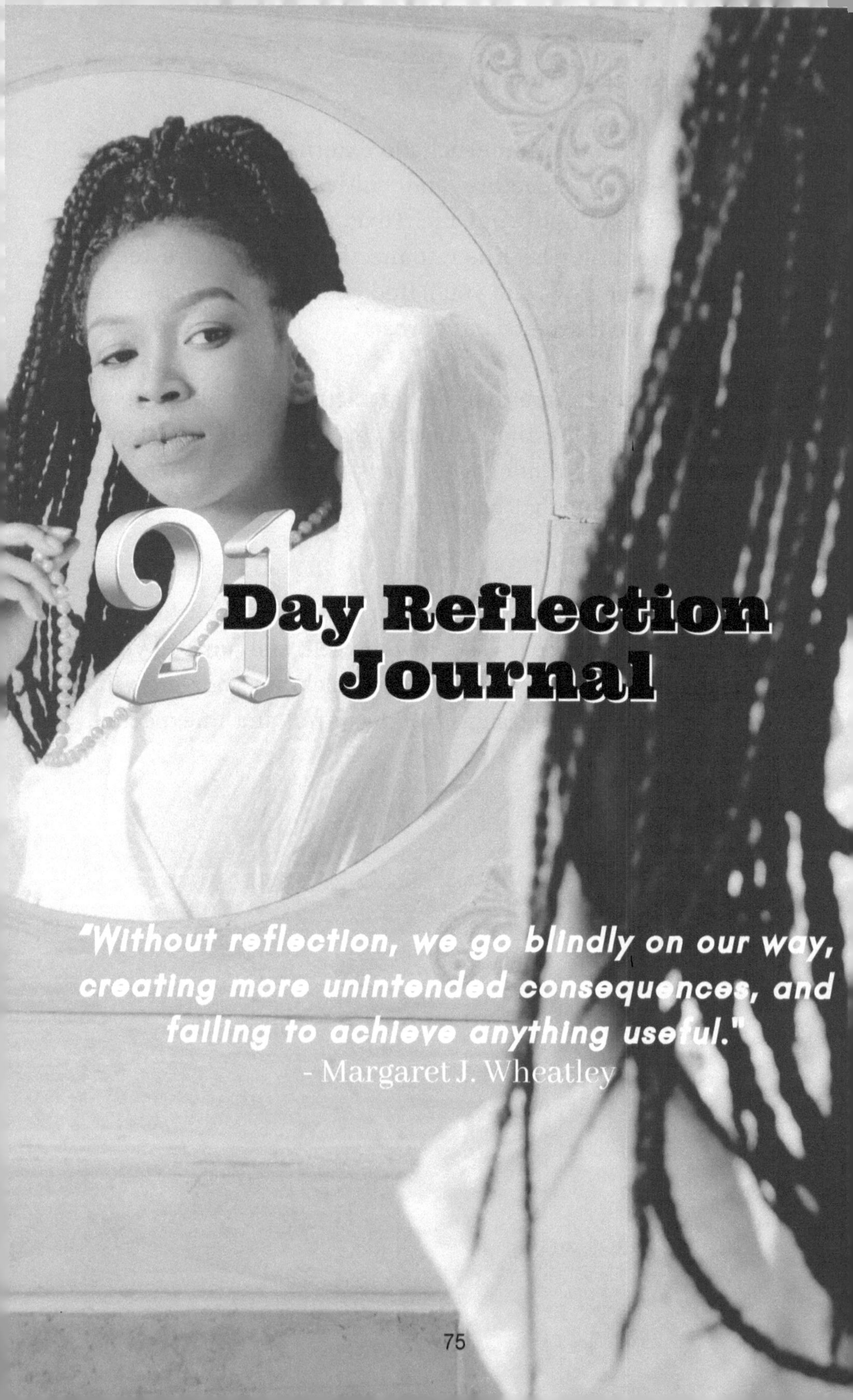

21 Day Reflection Journal

"Without reflection, we go blindly on our way, creating more unintended consequences, and failing to achieve anything useful."

- Margaret J. Wheatley

"You are allowed
to be both a masterpiece and a
work in progress.
simultaneously."

-UNKNOWN

Welcome to your 21-Day Reflection Journal

This journey is an opportunity for you to delve deep into your thoughts, emotions, and experiences, fostering a greater understanding of yourself and paving the way for personal growth and healing.

Reflection is a powerful tool that allows you to pause and look inward, to explore the nuances of your inner world, and to recognize patterns in your thoughts and behaviors. By dedicating time each day to this practice, you will uncover insights that can transform your life, providing clarity, peace, and a renewed sense of purpose.

Over the next 21 days, you will be guided through a series of prompts designed to help you navigate various aspects of your life—your past, your present, and your future. Each prompt is crafted to encourage honest introspection and to challenge you to confront the emotions and experiences that have shaped you.

Why 21 Days?

Research suggests that it takes approximately 21 days to form a new habit. By committing to this journal for the next three weeks, you are not only embarking on a journey of self-discovery but also cultivating a lasting habit of reflection that can benefit you long after this period ends.

What to Expect

Each day, you will be presented with a specific prompt or question that invites you to explore a different facet of your life. Some days may focus on acknowledging and processing past experiences, while others may encourage you to dream and plan for the future. There will also be prompts that center on your current state of being, helping you to ground yourself in the present moment.

How to Use This Journal

Create a Dedicated Space: Find a quiet, comfortable space where you can write without interruptions. This will be your sanctuary for reflection.

1. Set Aside Time: Dedicate a specific time each day for journaling. Consistency is key to forming a new habit and making the most of this experience.

2. Be Honest: Approach each prompt with an open mind and heart. Honest reflection is where true growth begins.

3. Take Your Time: There is no rush. Allow yourself the freedom to write as much or as little as you need. Some prompts may require more time and thought, and that's perfectly okay.

4. Revisit and Reflect: Periodically look back on your entries to see how your thoughts and feelings have evolved. This can provide valuable insights and reinforce your progress.

The Power of Reflection

Through this journaling journey, you will learn to listen to your inner voice, to validate your feelings, and to honor your experiences. Reflection can help you understand the root of your emotions, identify areas where you want to grow, and set meaningful goals for your future.

As you embark on this 21-day journey, remember to be kind to yourself. Reflection is not always easy, and it may bring up challenging emotions. But it is through this process that you can find healing, clarity, and a deeper connection to your true self.

Welcome to your journey of self-discovery and transformation. Take a deep breath, open your heart, and begin.

Setting Intentions

What are your intentions for this 21-day journey?
What do you hope to achieve or discover about
yourself?

____

____

____

____

____

____

____

____

____

____

____

____

____

____

____

____

____

____

Gratitude

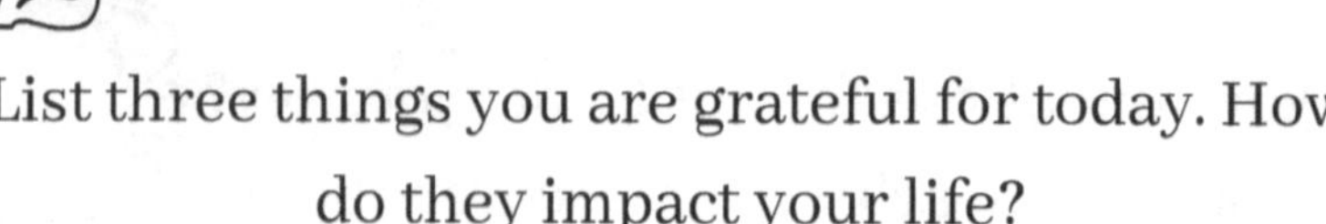

List three things you are grateful for today. How
do they impact your life?

Self-Awareness

Describe a recent situation where you felt a strong emotion (positive or negative). What triggered it, and how did you respond?

Energy and Vibration

How do you feel about your energy levels and overall
vibration? What changes can you make to enhance
your positive energy?

Betrayal and Trust

Describe a time you felt betrayed. How has this experience shaped your ability to trust others?

Lies and Truth

Reflect on a time you were lied to. How did it change your perception of the person and the situation?

7 Mistreatment and Resilience

Write about an instance where you were mistreated. How did you cope, and what did you learn from it??

Challenges and Obstacles

What are the biggest challenges you face right now? How can you overcome them or approach them differently?

Expressing Yourself

How can journaling help you express feelings you might otherwise suppress? Write freely about any current emotions.

10 **Releasing Resentment**

What resentments are you holding onto? How can you begin to release them?

Fear and Courage

What fears are holding you back? How can you
confront and overcome these fears with courage?

Letting Go

What do you need to let go of in your life to move forward? How can you start the process of letting go?

Seeking Peace

What does a peaceful life look like to you? What steps can you take to achieve it?

Personal Growth

How have you grown from your experiences of hurt? What strengths have you developed?

Inspirations and Role Models

Who inspires you and why? How can you incorporate their positive traits or actions into your life?

Self-Reflection

Reflect on a past mistake or regret. What did you learn from it, and how has it shaped you?

Compassion for Yourself

Write a letter of compassion to yourself.
Acknowledge your pain and offer yourself
kindness and understanding.

Kindness and Compassion

How can you practice more kindness and compassion towards yourself and others?

Visualization

Visualize your ideal life. Describe it in detail. What steps can you take to start making this vision a reality?

20

Future Goals

What are your short-term and long-term goals? How can you start working towards them today?

Reflection and Moving Forward

Reflect on your 21-day journey. What have you learned about yourself, and how will you continue to apply these insights in your life?